Find these items in the big picture.

Connect the dots from 1 to 5.

Decorate the gingerbread cookie. Give it a face!

1 Give it a Happy Face

2 Give it a Silly Face

3 Give it a Sleepy Face

Find these items in the big picture.

Circle the two Christmas trees with the same decorations.

Finish the picture of Santa.

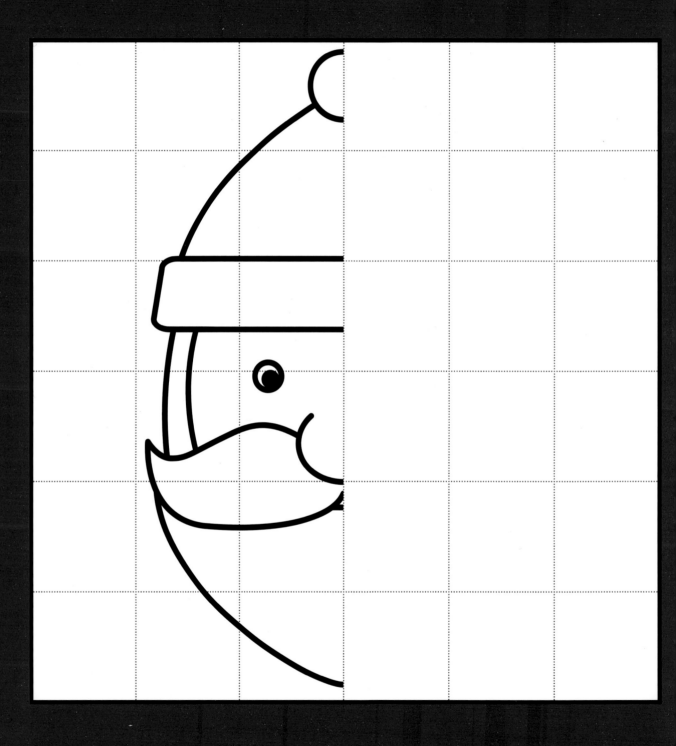

Count the hats, the scarves, and the gloves.
Write how many of each below.

Compare the sets in each pair. Circle the set that has **fewer**.

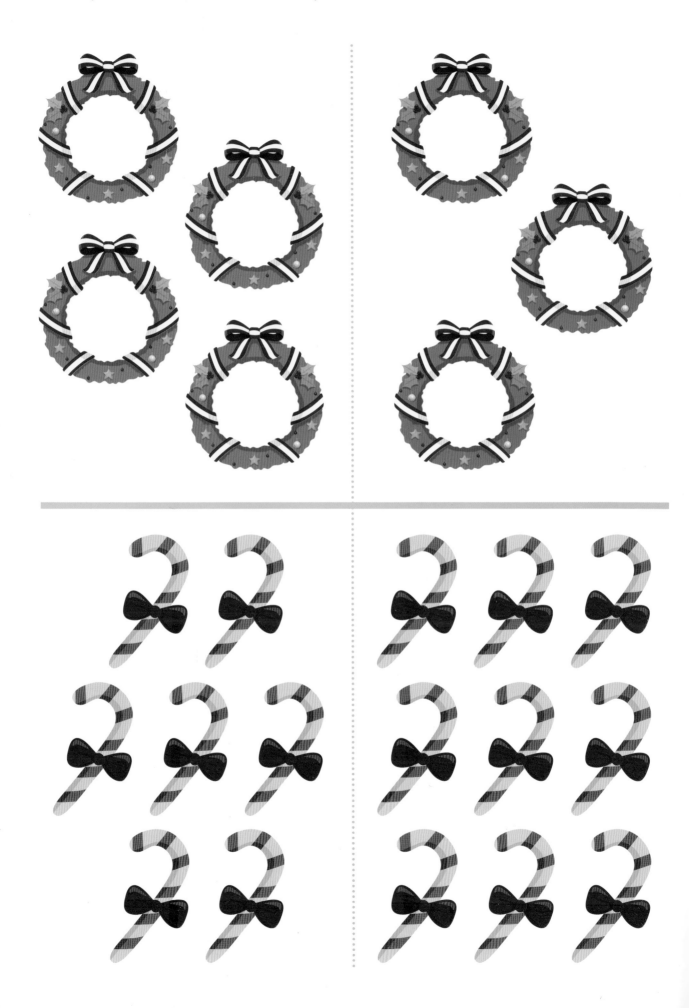

'Tis the Season

Find the following words in the puzzle.
Words are hidden → and ↓.

BELLS	CAROLS	CHRISTMAS	DECEMBER
FAMILY	HOLIDAY	JOY	MERRY

D	B	E	L	L	S	R	F	M	B	D
L	S	F	B	X	Z	F	A	G	Z	E
C	A	R	O	L	S	U	M	F	K	C
H	L	O	D	O	E	Q	I	E	V	E
R	C	M	Q	W	R	O	L	T	J	M
I	B	E	S	T	R	T	Y	M	C	B
S	Z	R	P	X	C	P	P	K	X	E
T	T	R	H	V	L	I	K	T	P	R
M	G	Y	E	I	J	M	J	U	W	F
A	I	S	A	H	O	L	I	D	A	Y
S	C	H	M	L	Y	Y	Z	X	Z	U

Draw an ornament! Follow the steps in the pictures.

Draw more ornaments on the Christmas tree.

Decorate the stocking. Write your name.

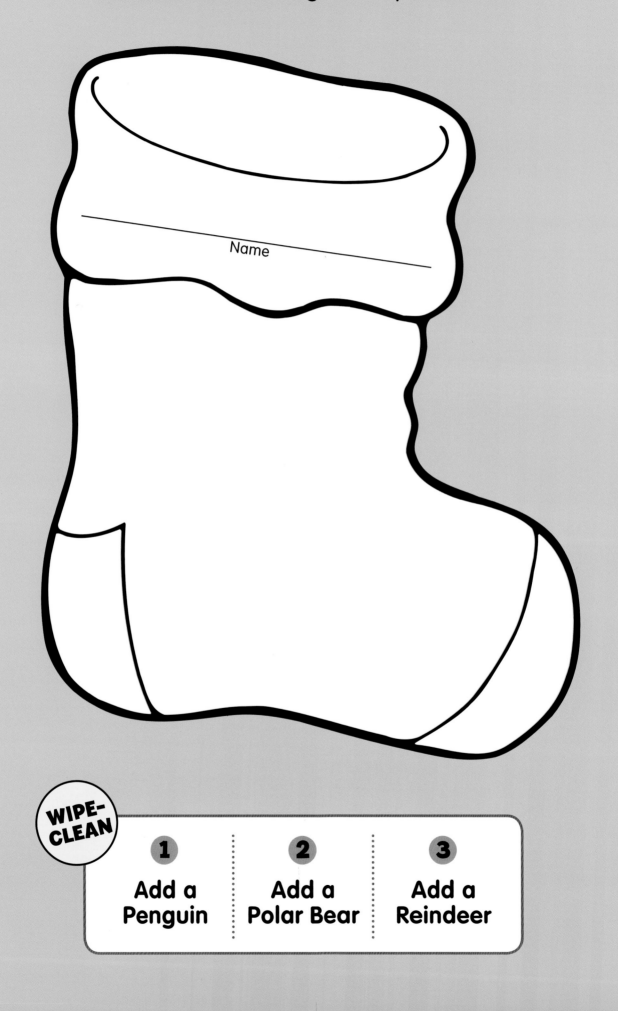

Name

WIPE-CLEAN

1 Add a Penguin

2 Add a Polar Bear

3 Add a Reindeer

Trace the path of each elf to a toy.

Holiday Scramble

Use the picture clues to unscramble each word.
The first one has been done for you.

FGIT

GIFT

STGINCKO

SLBEL

CEPIREAFL

SNTMEAORN

ROLCASRE

Find these items in the big picture.

Connect the dots from 1 to 10.

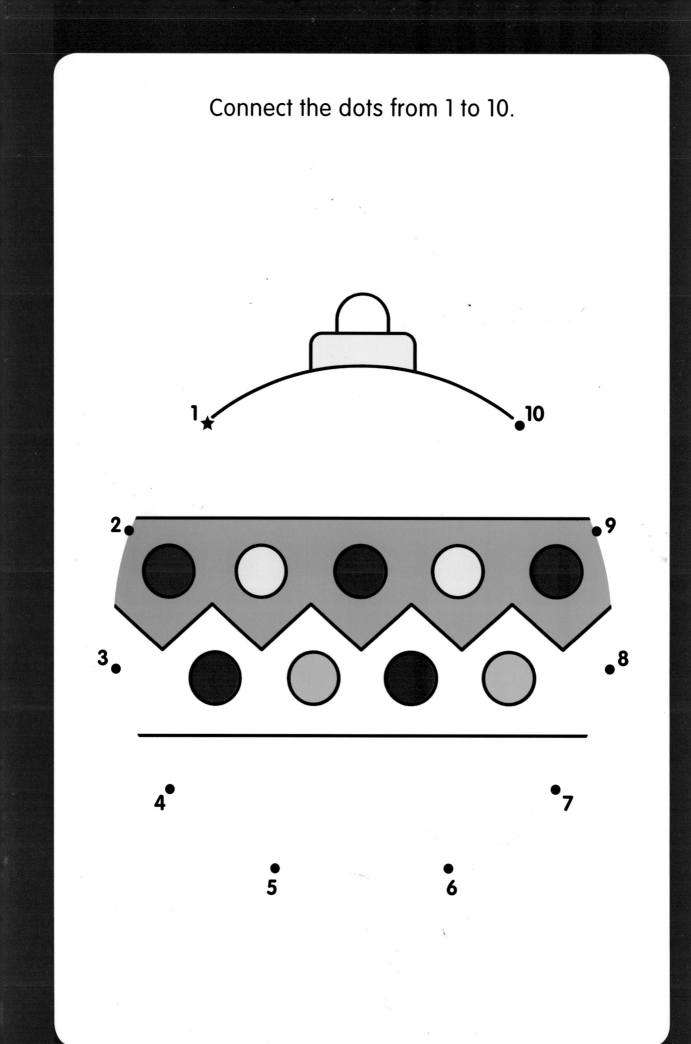

Help the boy find his friends.

Count each row. Write your answer in the box.

Make an invitation for your Christmas party.

WIPE-CLEAN

1 Draw Stars on the Card

2 Draw Santa on the Card

3 Draw Holly on the Card

Draw a snowman! Follow the steps in the pictures.

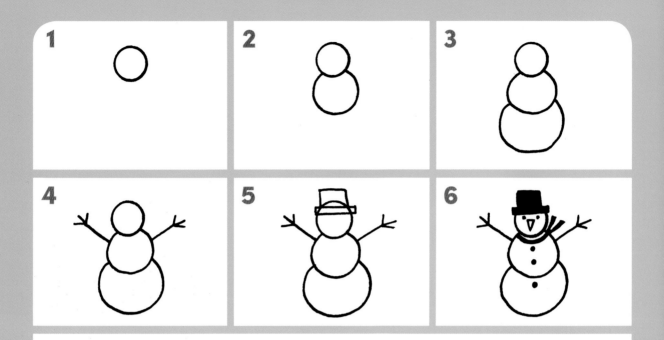

Draw more snowpeople.

Holiday Scramble

Use the picture clues to unscramble each word.
The first one has been done for you.

FYAMLI

FAMILY

YDCAN EACN

_____

RTAS

NTUCKRAERC

_____

FLE

HWTRAE

_____

Finish the picture of the reindeer.

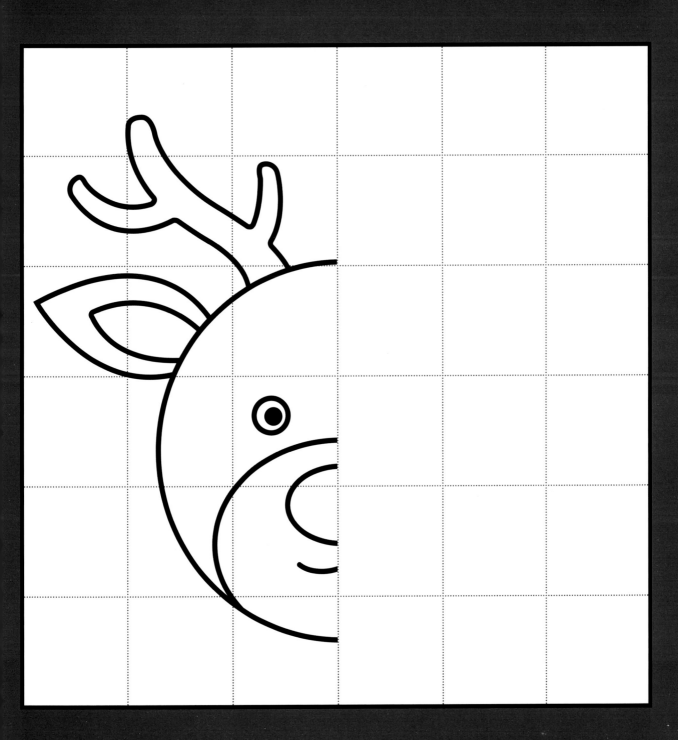

Connect the dots from 1 to 15.

Holiday Favorites

Find the following words in the puzzle.
Words are hidden ➡ and ⬇.

CANDY CANES   COOKIES   DECORATING   FRUITCAKE
GINGERBREAD   PRESENTS   PUDDING   WRAPPING

C	T	B	F	W	R	A	P	P	I	N	G
Q	Z	X	W	B	O	G	T	C	G	Z	G
F	R	U	I	T	C	A	K	E	T	Q	I
P	M	Y	A	O	C	N	Q	H	N	A	N
R	O	D	E	C	O	R	A	T	I	N	G
E	K	M	A	G	O	E	W	Y	Q	S	E
S	E	P	I	U	K	R	E	C	F	L	R
E	P	U	D	D	I	N	G	A	X	Q	B
N	M	L	Z	G	E	R	S	N	Y	T	R
T	L	K	Q	J	S	E	R	E	L	M	E
S	T	D	E	M	T	A	P	S	M	B	A
C	A	N	D	Y	C	A	N	E	S	Z	D

Help Santa get to the North Pole.

Circle the two sweaters with the same pattern.

Draw a face on the snowman. Add a scarf. Give it a hat.

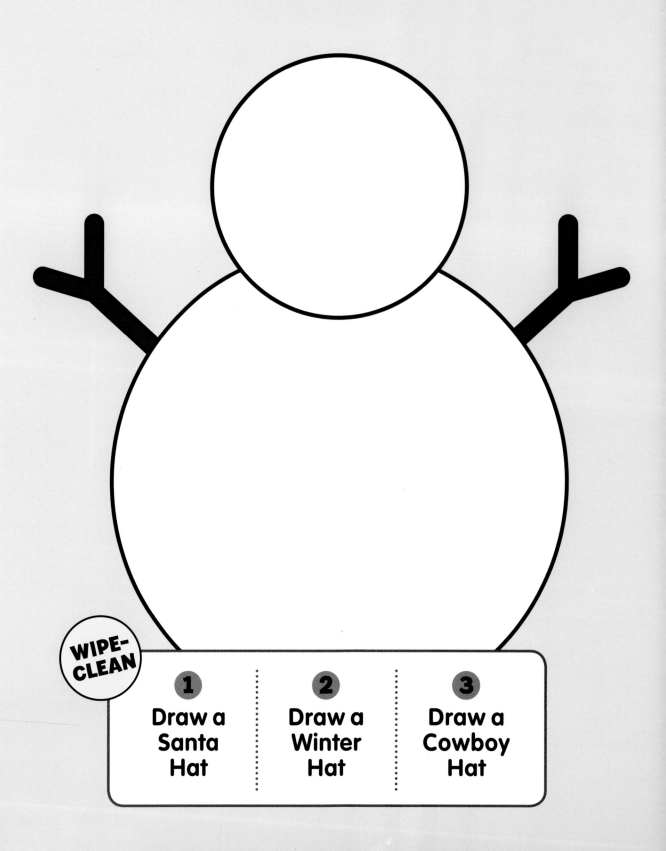

WIPE-CLEAN

1 Draw a Santa Hat

2 Draw a Winter Hat

3 Draw a Cowboy Hat

Count each row. Write your answer in the box.

Compare the sets in each pair. Circle the set that has more.

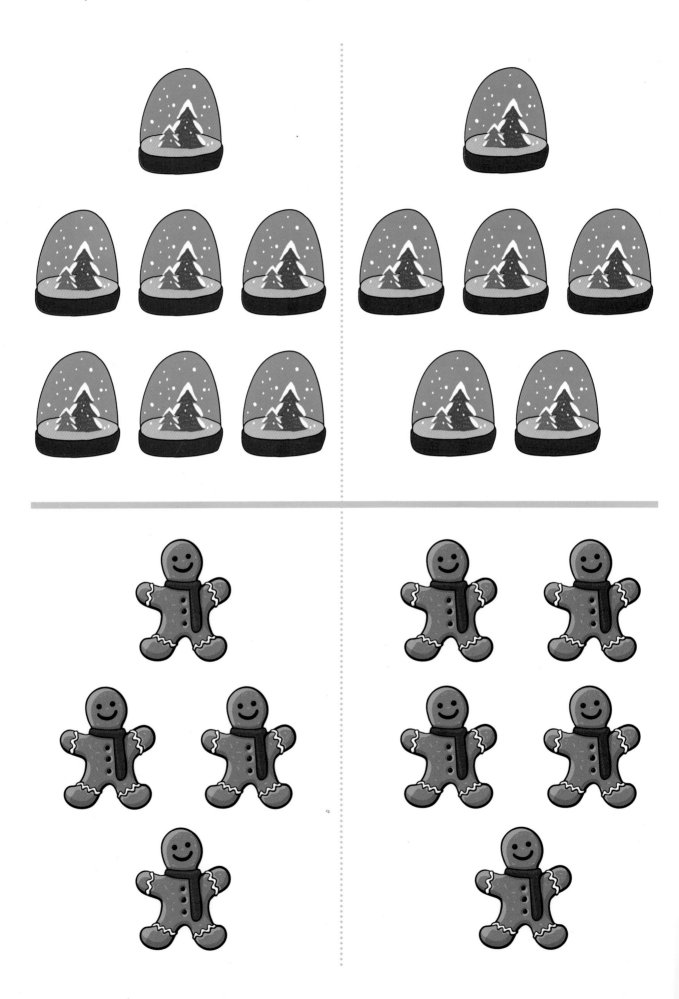

Design a postage stamp for your letter to Santa.

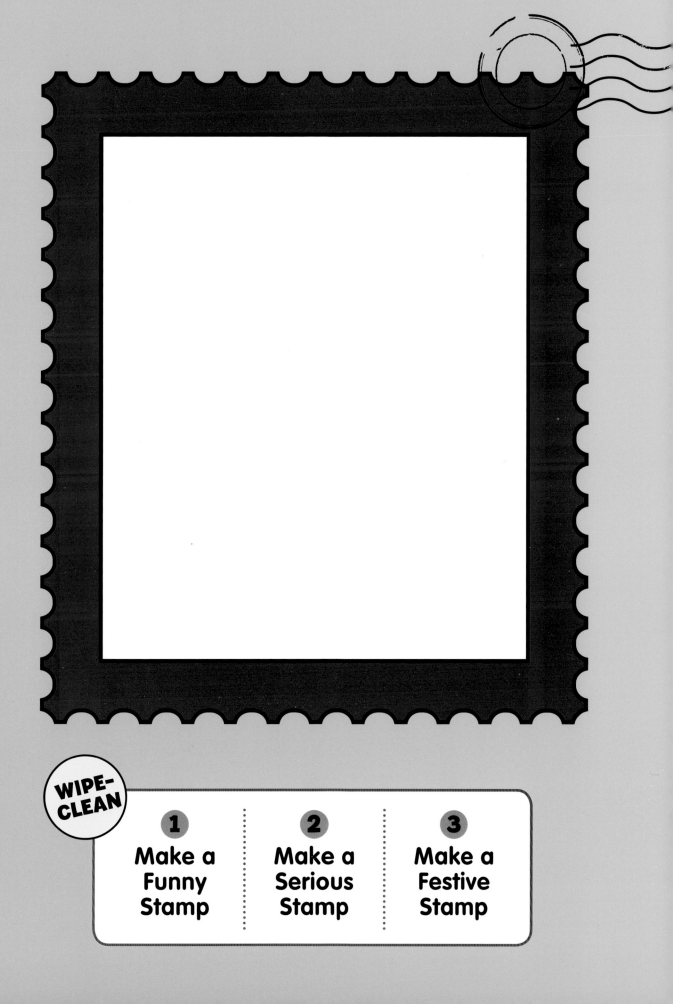

WIPE-CLEAN

1 Make a Funny Stamp

2 Make a Serious Stamp

3 Make a Festive Stamp

Draw a reindeer! Follow the steps in the pictures.

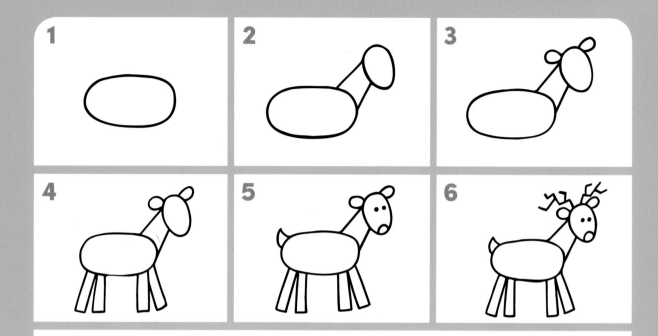

Draw more reindeer.

Finish the picture of the elf.

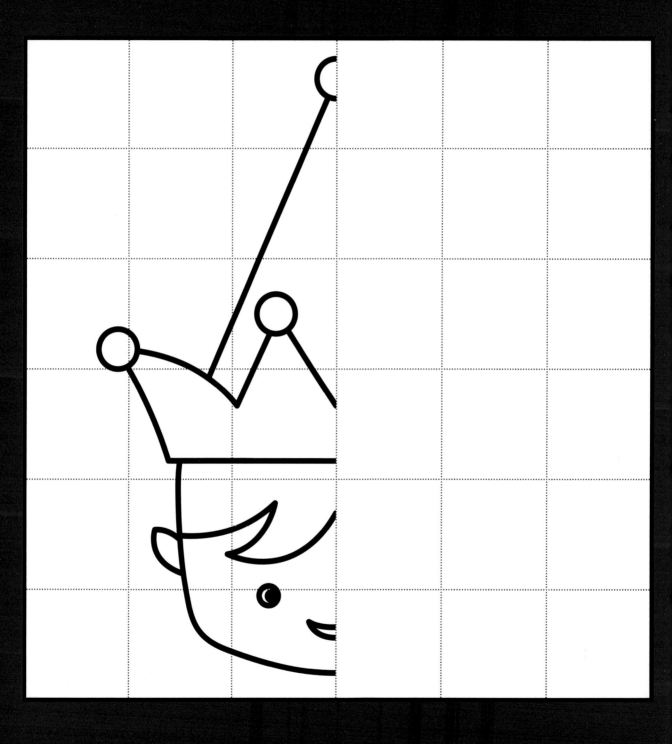

Help the elf get to Santa's workshop.

This is me on Christmas morning.

WIPE-CLEAN

1
Give Yourself Elf Ears

2
Give Yourself Antlers

3
Give Yourself a Santa Hat

Connect the dots from 1 to 22.

Trace Santa's path to each house.

Find these items in the big picture.

Let's Decorate!

Find the following words in the puzzle.
Words are hidden ➡ and ⬇.

ANGEL	CANDLES	GARLAND	HOLLY
LIGHTS	MISTLETOE	ORNAMENTS	STAR
STOCKING	TINSEL	TREE	WREATH

N L M S R O A Y S T A R

M I S T L E T O E L P Z

B G R O Y X T R S P T M

N H N C N R G N A T R Z

K T R K Q T Z A N G E L

U S I I T I T M S D E U

D M H N S N R E G H I W

E Z I G P S L N T O O R

Z L V K B E Z T L L Y E

H C A N D L E S W L J A

J B D S P Q R L K Y P T

G A R L A N D X T R J H

Count the number of each type of toy.
Write how many of each below.

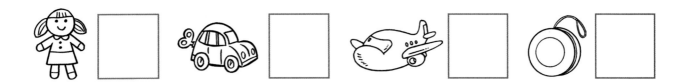

Design a holiday shopping bag.

WIPE-CLEAN

1 Draw Squares on the Bag

2 Draw Stripes on the Bag

3 Draw Circles on the Bag

Holiday Scramble

Use the picture clues to unscramble each word.
The first one has been done for you.

ERDENIRE

REINDEER

IELHGS

_____

LLOHY

_____

MNICHEY

_____

ATNSA

_____

ERTE

_____

Draw an angel! Follow the steps in the pictures.

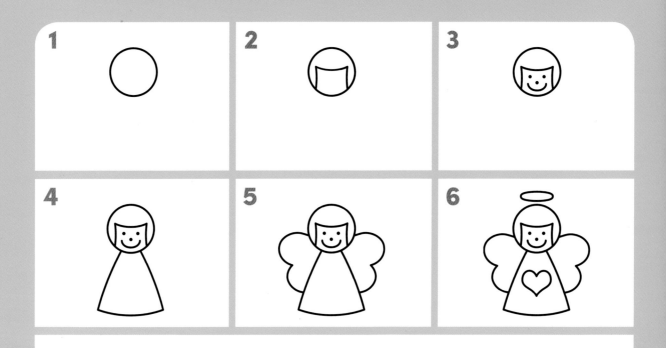

Draw more angels.

Finish the picture of the toy soldier.

Find the two gingerbread cookies that do not have a match.

Connect the dots from 1 to 30.

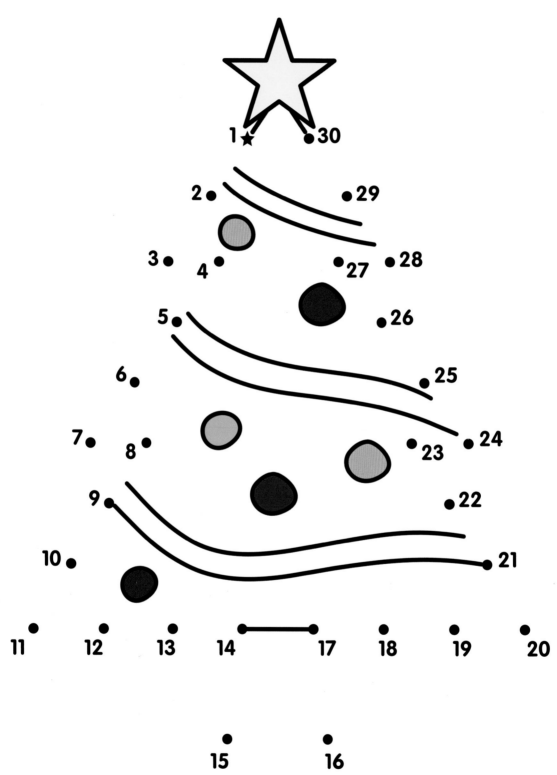

Find these items in the big picture.

Match each reindeer to its twin.

Draw wrapping paper on the gift box.

WIPE-CLEAN

1 Draw a Simple Design

2 Draw a Silly Design

3 Draw a Fancy Design

All About St. Nick

Find the following words in the puzzle.
Words are hidden ➡ and ⬇.

CHIMNEY	ELVES	GIFTS	JINGLE
LIST	NORTH POLE	REINDEER	RUDOLPH
SANTA	SLEIGH	TOYS	WINTER

L I S T D T C I T D R
F J N O R T H P O L E
Q W M T U H I V Y V I
R I L P D T M H S H N
E N H R O G N J D J D
G T B Z L U E J O I E
I E L W P E Y U T N E
F R T M H F X Q X G R
T X S L E I G H Y L G
S A N T A Z E L V E S

Skip count by 2s to connect the dots.

Draw an elf! Follow the steps in the pictures.

Draw more elves.

Help the children find their way to the house.